IMAGES
of America

COLCHESTER

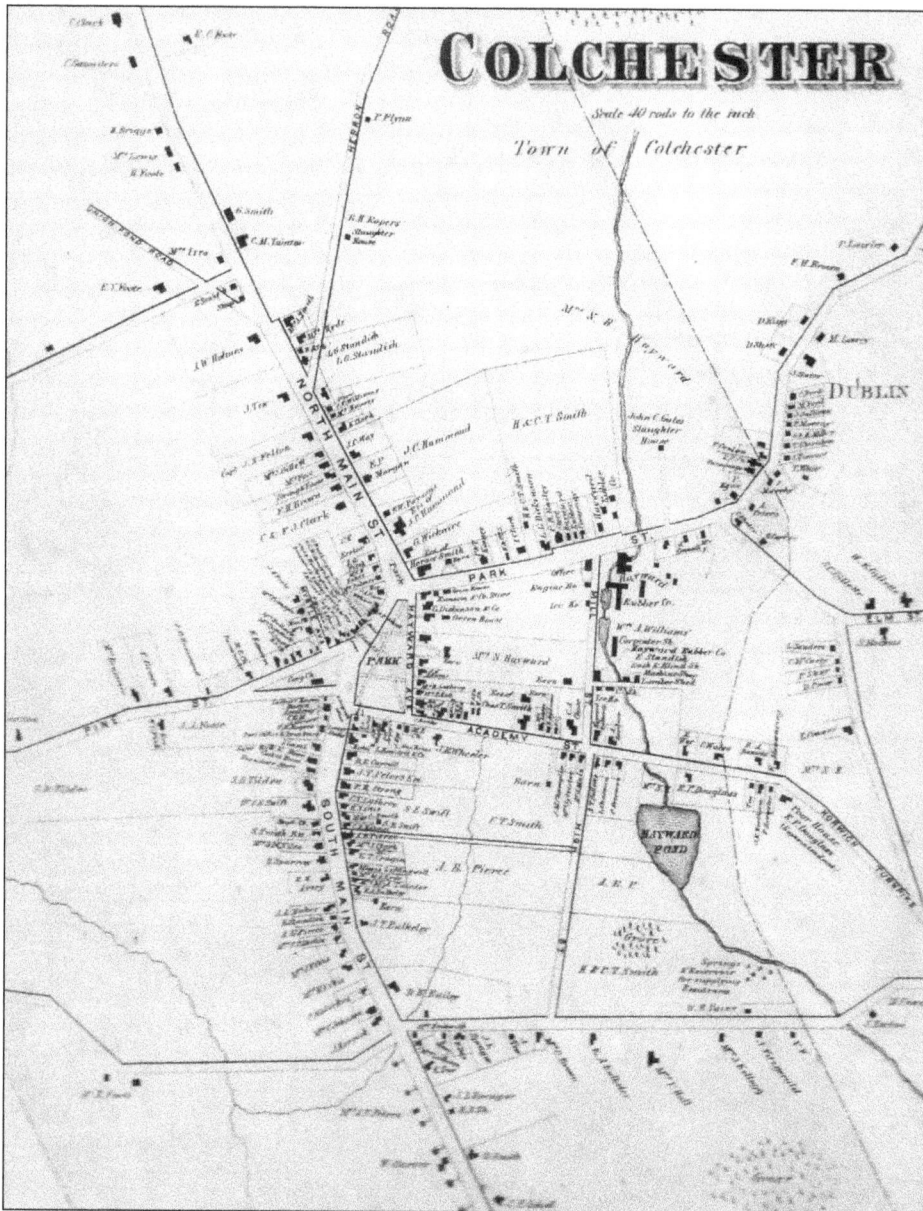

This is a portion of an 1868 map of Colchester from the *Atlas of New London County, Connecticut*, by F.W. Beers (published by F.W. Beers, A.D. Ellis, and C.G. Soule in Philadelphia in 1868). Note that many of the street names in Colchester have changed, including Hebron Road (now Amston Road), North Main Street (Broadway), Park Street (Lebanon Avenue), Pine Street (Linwood Avenue), and High Street (Pleasant Street). In this book, modern street names will be used unless otherwise noted. (Courtesy of the Colchester Historical Society.)

ON THE COVER: This view looks south along Main Street, locally known as Merchants' Row. The edge of the town green is visible at left. The Colchester Congregational Church is in the background between the trees. The building on the right is the last one on the north end of Merchants' Row. The Colchester Historical Society possesses the original glass plate negative of this photograph, which dates to between 1888 and 1890. (Courtesy of the Colchester Historical Society.)

IMAGES
of America

COLCHESTER

Gary A. Walter on behalf
of the Colchester Historical Society
Foreword by Arthur S. Liverant

ARCADIA
PUBLISHING

Published by Arcadia Publishing
Charleston, South Carolina

Library of Congress Control Number: 2020940235

For all general information, please contact Arcadia Publishing:
Telephone 843-853-2070
Fax 843-853-0044
E-mail sales@arcadiapublishing.com
For customer service and orders:
Toll-Free 1-888-313-2665

Visit us on the Internet at www.arcadiapublishing.com

This photograph of Colchester Falls was taken in May 1889 by local photographer Cortis F. McIntosh (1851–1923). The Colchester Historical Society has the actual 8-by-10-inch glass plate negative from which this print was made. Colchester Falls still exists but is now on private property near Falls Circle off Bulkeley Hill Road. (Courtesy of the Colchester Historical Society.)

CONTENTS

FOREWORD

As is often quoted, "a picture is worth a thousand words." Gary Walter has done a masterful job in choosing the photographs that convey the colorful story of Colchester, Connecticut, from the late 19th century until the mid-1950s. Fortunately, Colchester had several early photographers who were fascinated by the technology that could freeze time and record real history for future generations. The fortunate recipients are the citizens and historians of our town who have the opportunity to look back to the years of a slower life and architecture that reflects a prospering New England town founded in 1698. Walter highlights buildings that have survived the events of the 18th and 19th centuries, including winter blizzards, devastating hurricanes, and northeasters, which flooded the lowlands of New London County.

Colchester is located in the crossroads of Connecticut and reflects the influx of diverse peoples of various ethnicities, including Native American, Irish, African American, Italian, Jewish, Russian, Polish, and Eastern European. This melting pot makes Colchester the charming, historic, and progressive place—originally named for the ancient Roman town of Colchester, England—that has led our citizens to love and cherish it.

Gary Walter has sifted through and chosen a broad range of photographs to give the reader a glimpse of the success of the experiment of the new people in a new land. The motto "Where Tradition Meets Tomorrow" is appropriate and is a goal we pursue in our quest to make Colchester a destination. Gary is obviously proud of Colchester, and his photographic history demonstrates his enthusiasm.

—Arthur Liverant

ACKNOWLEDGMENTS

The day that I was voted on to the Colchester Historical Society Board of Governors, they were also looking to find someone to start up and chair a Collections Committee, and I volunteered to do it. The officers and board of the society have never failed to support this committee's work, which has made it possible to identify and locate the images needed for this book from the society's collections.

I would specifically like to thank the president of the society, Mary Tomasi, and past presidents Gigi Liverant and Angela George. I would also like to thank Sheila Tortorigi for being willing to take over the Collections Committee chairmanship from me and continue and expand the committee's work; she is doing an outstanding job. I would also like to thank my fellow board member and Colchester native Arthur Liverant for being willing to review my text and images for accuracy and for writing the foreword for this book. I would also like to acknowledge the late Barbara Woods Brown, who, decades ago, did the monumental task of compiling the real estate records for many of the properties in central Colchester; these records were instrumental in the writing of this book.

I would like to thank William Farrell, who, for years, has graciously contributed his photographic expertise to the Colchester Historical Society Collections Committee. I would also like to thank—and dedicate this book to—my wife, Kathleen Wallace-Walter, who is a retired information technology professional, for the technical assistance, not to mention the encouragement that she provided while I was writing this book and for the last 30-plus years. I would also like to thank Caitrin Cunningham, my title manager at Arcadia Publishing, for her invaluable guidance during the writing and editing of this book.

With the exception of the image of the Colchester Historical Society Museum on page 127, all of the photographs in this book came from the collections of the Colchester Historical Society. One item in the society's collection not only provided many images used in this book but also their context: the photograph album owned by Ronald K. Brown, who systematically photographed or compiled photographs of most of the buildings in Colchester in the late 19th and early 20th centuries. His mother was Harriet Parsons, a native of Colchester, who married a New York lawyer named Joseph Brown and moved to Manhattan with him. Ronald was born in Manhattan in 1863 and lived and worked there as a lawyer for most of his life. However, his mother had inherited a house on Broadway in Colchester, which the family used as a summer residence into the 1940s, when Ronald is thought to have died. His photograph album was donated to the Colchester Historical Society in 1964.

—Gary A. Walter
Colchester, Connecticut
May 2020

INTRODUCTION

The purpose of this book is to convey a sense of what Colchester, Connecticut, looked like in the late 19th and early 20th centuries through photographs from the Colchester Historical Society's collections. Colchester was incorporated in 1698 as a typical New England farming community. During the Revolutionary War, Connecticut got the nickname "the Provision State" because it provided supplies and food to the Continental army in larger proportion to its size than other states. In Colchester, state commissary Col. Henry Champion was one of the primary contributors to this effort.

By 1800, Colchester was quite prosperous, with Pierpoint and Abigail Bacon being among the town's wealthiest residents. They both died in 1800, and in Pierpoint's will, he bequeathed his entire estate to the town to build a school. This school opened in 1803 and was named Bacon Academy in his honor. The school was unique in the state, as it not only provided what would now be called primary education but also secondary and college-preparatory education. In essence, Bacon Academy was the state's first high school.

Another unprecedented aspect of education in Colchester at the time Bacon Academy opened was the creation of the School for Colored Children. One of the special things about this school was that the African American students were taught by African American teachers. In 1842, Bacon Academy began to admit females to its higher education branches, and in 1848, the school was racially integrated more than a century before *Brown v. Board of Education* led to the official end of segregation across the rest of the United States.

Colchester also has a unique industrial history. There are two essential steps needed to make vulcanized rubber. One is to treat the raw rubber with sulfur, a process that Nathaniel Hayward discovered and patented. The second is to heat the sulfur-treated rubber to a precise temperature for a specific time period, which Charles Goodyear discovered. Hayward and Goodyear were associates, and in 1838, they made an agreement that resulted in the vulcanized rubber patent being issued in Goodyear's name, while Hayward received a license to make vulcanized rubber footwear products.

In 1847, Hayward decided to build a rubber factory in Colchester. It opened the following year and was called the Hayward Rubber Company. This was a large-scale and successful operation, which typically employed more than 600 people and produced thousands of shoe and boot products per day. The factory promoted prosperity and growth in the town for decades until it started having major problems by the 1880s and was suddenly closed without warning at the end of 1893. The closure caused the biggest population and economic crash in the history of Colchester, triggering the mass abandonment of houses, businesses, and farms. Around the start of the 20th century, all of this inexpensive real estate led to an influx of new people who created new types of businesses that eventually led to the revitalization of the town.

In the first half of the 20th century, the hotel and resort business—owned mostly by and catering to Jewish people—became particularly important in Colchester. This business was so successful that Colchester acquired the nickname "the Catskills of Connecticut." Colchester can also be proud of being the lifelong home of World War II Congressional Medal of Honor winner William J. Johnston, who passed away in 1990. Today, Colchester is again prosperous, and appropriately, the town's motto is "Where Tradition Meets Tomorrow."

One

INFRASTRUCTURE

STREETS, TOWN GREEN, AND RAILROAD STATION

The transportation backbone connecting Colchester to the rest of Connecticut since the beginning was the Hartford and New London Road. The portion in the center of town—which now consists of Old Hebron Road, Broadway, Main Street, and South Main Street—was originally known as Towne Street.

Roads that connected to the surrounding towns were authorized at town meetings, and committees were created to build these roads, which were all unpaved at the time. In the 19th century, the state chartered turnpike corporations to take control of many of these roads and charge fees for their use. The turnpikes in Colchester and the year in which each was chartered are as follows: Hartford and New London Turnpike, 1800; Colchester and Norwich Turnpike, 1805; Colchester and Chatham Turnpike, 1808; and East Haddam and Colchester Turnpike, 1809. Many of the roads still in use today date back to these old turnpikes.

Until 1877, the only public conveyance available to anyone traveling to or from Colchester was a stagecoach; that year, the Colchester Railroad Company completed a three-and-a-half-mile spur into Colchester from the Airline Railroad. This company serviced both the Hayward Rubber Company (where the spur terminated) and the general public at passenger and freight depots on what is now Lebanon Avenue. Passenger service to Colchester ended in the 1950s, and freight service ended in the 1960s. The tracks were removed, and the railbed is now part of the Air Line State Park Trail.

What is now the town green was originally the property of Dudley Wright, the builder of the house now known as the Hayward House. In 1805, a private driveway was built where Hayward Avenue is now located, surrounding what is now the town green with roads. In 1821, Dr. John R. Watrous, David Deming, and Ralph Isham bought what is now the southern half of the green and sold it to the Bacon Academy Board of Trustees, which still owns it. The northern part of the green was donated to the Borough of Colchester in 1851 by Nathaniel Hayward, and as part of the arrangement, what is now Hayward Avenue became a public road named after him.

The original settlement of Colchester started in the area where the recreation complex and Chanticlair Golf Course are located on Old Hebron Road. The original home lot that now encompasses the golf course was granted to Josiah Strong in 1704. The house at 288 Old Hebron Road was built about 1904 by Hamilton Wallis, a New Jersey judge, who purchased the property in 1902. This was the Wallis summer home for many years. The 90-acre property was rented to tenants, including Morris Stollman, a Russian immigrant, who operated a poultry farm on it starting in the 1930s. In 1944, Stollman purchased the house and property. Eventually, his son Hyman became the owner of the property and, in the early 1970s, built the Chanticlair Golf Course on the land. The house and water tower are both still standing.

Chas Clark place - Later Mrs - A'he

What is now the recreation complex on the southwest side of Old Hebron Road was the site of the original home lot of Ebenezer Skinner, granted in 1705. In 1848, Charles Clark purchased the property; by 1850, he had built the house shown in these two photographs. The property stayed in the Clark family until 1897. In 1918, Abraham Lapping and his wife, Anna, who were Jewish immigrants from Latvia, bought the property. For decades, they operated a dairy farm on it. By the 1960s, both Abraham and Anna Lapping had passed away, and their son sold the property to the town. The house was probably taken down about this time. Old Hebron Road was not paved until around 1934; therefore, the below photograph showing it as a dirt road must date to earlier.

Cha' Clark place later mrs. Clark Clark

The home lot where the town tennis courts are now located was originally granted to Thomas Day in 1705. In 1931, Mr. and Mrs. Constantine DeNora purchased 30 acres of the property, including the 19th-century farmhouse shown in these photographs. The DeNoras were immigrants from Italy. In Colchester, they started out as dairy farmers but eventually switched to poultry farming. The DeNoras were not the only ones in the poultry business at that time. One book about Connecticut farming called Colchester the "Egg Capital of New England." When the DeNoras started their farm, there were several other poultry farms on Old Hebron Road. When their son Michael and daughter-in-law Anne DeNora closed the business in 1995, it was the end of one of the last family-owned commercial poultry farms in town. The house is now gone.

The home lot on the west side of Old Hebron Road that includes the property in the photograph was granted to Jonathan Northam in 1715. This property changed hands numerous times over the decades, but in the 20th century, this house was known as the Munson House. This photograph dates to before 1930. The house is now gone.

This is another one of the original home lots in Colchester. The house shown in the photograph was on the southwest side of Old Hebron Road near what is now the intersection with Renee Drive. In 1875, Ralph Jones bought this property. In the 20th century, it was known as the Leal House. This house is now gone.

The area where the Colchester Hayward Fire Company Headquarters now stands at the junction of Old Hebron and Old Hartford Roads was originally part of the home lot granted to Josiah Gillett in 1703. The house shown in the photograph was built in 1842 by Frederick Rand, who bought the property in 1841. In 1909, the property and house were sold to Helen Lilienthal of Astoria, New York. In 1948, she changed her name to Helen Lonsdale, and the house became known as the Lonsdale House. In 1962, the property was sold, and the house was torn down. In 1980, the Schuster family donated the land to the town, and in 1985, a referendum was passed that allowed for the building of the fire station and headquarters. Construction of the station was started in 1986 by the firemen themselves, and it was dedicated in 1989.

The Georgian-style house at 191 Broadway, just below the junction of Old Hebron and Old Hartford Roads, is the site of the original home lot granted to Nathaniel Foote in 1707. This was not the Nathaniel Foote considered the founder of Colchester, who died in 1703, but rather his eldest son. The house that still stands on this lot was built about 1785 and is referred to as the Foote Family House. In 1767, Nathaniel Foote transferred the property to his son Daniel—who is probably the one responsible for having it built, not Nathaniel, who died in 1774. The house is also known as the Strong or Bock House (after later owners). Broadway was first paved around 1927; therefore, this photograph must date to before then. Do not confuse this house with the DAR-Foote House, which was originally somewhere on Old Hebron Road but is now on Norwich Avenue. The DAR-Foote House is where Nathaniel Foote (1682–1774) and his family actually lived.

The house in this photograph was on the west side of Broadway, south of the Foote Family House, and was known as the Tew House. Colchester's land records show that Gilbert Tew acquired the house and property in 1886. By the 1960s, the house had been subdivided into several apartments, and over the following years, it had deteriorated considerably. In 1973, all of the tenants were notified that the house was to be demolished, and they had to relocate. The owner of the house at this time was David Hurwit, who had been a longtime Colchester firefighter; presumably because of this, he donated the house to the town for the use of the fire company. Therefore, in April 1975, the house was burned to the ground as part of a training exercise for the Colchester Hayward Fire Company.

It is not known when the building in this photograph was erected. It was located on the west side of Broadway south of the Tew House. This building is known to have been used as an annex to the Fairview House Hotel next door on Broadway. The building was removed or torn down after 1991. The photograph is dated 1924.

The building at 119 Broadway, across from Harry's Place, was built around 1808 as a residence for John Sparrow. In 1869, the Hayward Rubber Company bought the house and converted it to be used as boarding space for its single female employees. In 1919, the building started being used as the Fairview House Hotel, and this photograph dates to sometime after that. This structure is now used as an office building.

This house on the west side of Broadway, south of the Sparrow House, was referred to as the Watrous House. Colchester's land records show that this house was willed to Agnes Watrous, wife of John Watrous of East Hampton, in 1930. The photograph probably dates to before that time. This house is no longer standing.

This is a view of Broadway looking south from approximately where the Fairview House is now located. The house in the foreground at right is the Watrous House. Note that the road appears to be dirt. Broadway was paved around 1927, so this photograph must date to before that time.

This 19th-century house on the west side of Broadway at what is now the north corner of Clark Lane was known over the course of its existence as the Turner, Clark, or Roper House. The house and property were purchased by J. Perry Klein in 1909, and the house was torn down shortly after that sale.

Soon after tearing down the house shown in the photograph at the top of this page, Dr. J. Perry Klein built the large Craftsman-style house shown in this image. It still stands at 71 Broadway and has been converted for commercial use; the building is currently home to a wine and spirits store.

Dr Robinson (D. W. Williams)

Dr Myron Robinson

The status of the house at 43 Broadway on the south side of Clark Lane has been in dispute. However, just before this book went to press in August 2020, the house was demolished. Research conducted as part of the dispute has indicated that it was built between 1797 and 1801 rather than in 1816, as was previously thought. The house was known as the Coggeshell-Robinson House after two of the families that owned it.

This photograph shows Dr. Myron W. Robinson (1839–1912), who enlisted in the US Army as a private during the Civil War but was quickly commissioned as a surgeon and served for three years in that position. Sometime after the war, he came to Colchester, where he had a medical practice for 24 years. He bought the Coggeshell-Robinson House in 1881 and owned it until 1905.

This unusually shaped house was located where a parking lot is now, south of Clark Lane. It was known as the Wickwire House after prominent local businessman Giles G. Wickwire, who owned the house in the late 19th century. The house was torn down in the 1980s. The photograph is dated 1903.

This view of Broadway looking north was taken from near the junction of Lebanon Avenue and Broadway. The house in the foreground at left is the Wickwire House. Note that Broadway in this photograph is still dirt, therefore, the photograph must have been taken before 1927, when the road was paved.

This grand three-story mansion was commissioned sometime between 1768 and 1788 by Jonathan Deming, an officer in the Continental army during the Revolutionary War. He was also a wealthy local businessman. It is thought that the person who built this house was Isaac Fitch, a noted local builder from neighboring Lebanon. The house stood on the south end of Broadway adjacent to Merchants' Row, about where Cragin Court and part of a parking lot is now. It was later owned by the Samuel P. Willard family and was known as the Deming-Willard House. Surprisingly, before this house was torn down in December 1957 to make way for a commercial development, the parlor of the house was somehow removed and transported to Bath, England, where it was reassembled and has been on display there, in the American Museum, ever since. This photograph dates to the early 20th century.

The above image shows the elegant entry hallway and stairway to the second floor of the Deming-Willard House on the west side of Broadway adjacent to Merchants' Row. The date of the photograph is unknown, but it was probably taken not long before the house was emptied and torn down in December 1957. The below image shows the first-floor drawing room on the north front side of the Deming-Willard House. Note the tiles around the fireplace and the fine paneling of the mantel and wall. This picture was taken shortly before the house was torn down.

This is a view of the east side of Broadway looking south. The building in the left foreground is the Jaffe Overlook Hotel, which still exists as an apartment building at 116 Broadway. South of the hotel is the Way House. This photograph must have been taken after 1927, when Broadway was first paved, and before the early 1930s, when the Way House was removed and Harry's Place was moved onto that site.

The Way House was built sometime before 1840. It was similar in style to the Trumbull House to its south and to the Watrous House on the west side of Broadway. All three houses had gambrel roofs, dormer windows, and a central entry door. This house was removed by the early 1930s, when the Harry's Place building was moved to this location.

The house standing next to Harry's Place at 80 Broadway was built between 1790 and 1801 by Benjamin Trumbull, who was a judge. His son Lyman was born in this house. After Lyman graduated from Bacon Academy, he left Colchester and eventually became a US senator, representing Illinois from 1855 to 1873. At the end of the Civil War, he coauthored the 13th Amendment to the US Constitution, which abolished slavery.

This image is of the east side of Broadway looking north, with the Trumbull House in the foreground and the Way House in the background. This photograph probably dates to the early 20th century. The Trumbull House, located at 80 Broadway, is also known as the Rose House (after a later owner) and the Butternot Cottage (for unknown reasons).

The house at 52 Broadway was built by Dr. Ezekiel Parsons around 1842. In 1868, Ezekiel's daughter Harriet (Parsons) Brown inherited the house. She lived in New York City with her husband and children, but the family used this house as their summer residence until 1942, when Harriet's son Ronald K. Brown finally sold it. Ronald K. Brown owned the photograph album—now in the Colchester Historical Society's collection—from which about seventy photographs in this book originated. The above photograph shows the original configuration of the house before it was extensively altered as shown in the below photograph. The dates when these photographs were taken are unknown.

Built about 1842

HAKES.

The house in this photograph was on the east side of Broadway in front of the site where a rehabilitation facility is now located. Joseph Churchill Hammond, one of the officers of the Hayward Rubber Company, bought the property in 1853. Hammond hired local builders Erastus Standish and John Wightman to build this large and impressive house, which they finished in 1855. The cupola alone was impressive enough that the *Hartford Evening Post* reported in its December 1874 edition that "J.C. Hammond's cupola, with its stained glass windows, was brilliantly illuminated." In 1883, the property was sold to Dwight and Lucy Hakes, and their family lived in the house until 1913. The Hammond-Hakes House was converted into an apartment building and used as such until it became dilapidated and was vacated and torn down in 1988.

Willard (Rev S. G.) House

The large house at 24 Broadway, which faces the small triangular extension of the town green, was built before 1771. The above photograph shows how it looked in the late 19th century with four large pillars in front; Rev. Samuel G. Willard, who served as the eighth pastor of the Colchester Congregational Church from 1868 to his death in 1887, owned the house at that time. After his wife died in 1896, the house was inherited by their daughter Mary, who was the wife of Dr. Edwin B. Cragin, who was born and raised in Colchester and went on to become a prominent New York City physician. Around the turn of the 20th century, the Cragins extensively altered the house, which they used as their summer residence, by adding a broad veranda, as shown in the below photograph.

The Willard house after alteration

The corner house before alteration

The elegant house at 12 Broadway on the corner of Lebanon Avenue was built on the site where the first tavern in Colchester, the Taintor Tavern, was located. The house was built in the 1840s. In 1867, Horace Smith bought the house, and the above photograph shows how the house looked around that time. Horace and his brother Charles owned a large farm south of Colchester. In 1899, Ardelia Cragin, a widow and the mother of Dr. Edwin B. Cragin, bought this property after her house on Linwood Avenue burned down in the Merchants' Row fire of 1898. The Cragin family owned the house until 1923, during which time the house was greatly altered, as shown in the below photograph. It is also worth noting that the first telephone switchboard in Colchester operated from here starting in the 1890s.

after alteration

This is the oldest known photograph of Main Street, which is locally known as Merchants' Row. The picture dates to 1873 and shows the southern half of Merchants' Row in the background and the northwestern portion of the town green in the foreground. The building on the far left is the Strong Block, which housed the general store of W.J.P. Strong, for whom the building is named. The building next to the Strong Block is the Pierce Block, named after its owner, Alfred Pierce. The first floor of this building was rented to the jeweler Isaac C. Gleason until 1874. The third building from the left is the Avery Block, named after its owner, George Avery. This building housed a saloon and a barbershop. These first three buildings survived the Merchants' Row fire of December 1, 1882; the remaining buildings shown here did not. The Strong Block also survived the Merchants' Row fire of 1890—but not the fire of 1898.

This 1888 photograph of Merchants' Row shows much of the same area as the 1873 photograph on the previous page. The picture was taken between the Merchants' Row fires of 1882 and 1890. The Pierce and Avery Blocks on the left are present and essentially unchanged from the 1873 photograph, but the rest of the structures have been rebuilt. The third building from the left is the Kellogg and Foote Block, named after owners Samuel Kellogg and Joseph Foote. The signs on the building's facade read "The Colchester Advocate" and "W.B. Otis." The next building to the right is the Adams Block, named after Joseph N. Adams, who owned it from 1862 until his death in 1906. This building's signs read "J.N. Adams" and "Savings Bank." The next building is the Worthington Block, named after Olcott Worthington, who owned it for 48 years. Note that at this time, the building consisted of three stories. The last two buildings on the right are the Scholl and Roper Blocks, named after John Scholl and Benjamin Roper.

This photograph shows the aftermath of the June 9, 1890, Merchants' Row fire. The undamaged building on the left—at the south end of Merchants' Row—is the Strong Block. The ruins on the far right are that of the Worthington, Scholl, and Roper Blocks, along with the ruins of the other buildings in between them.

Worthington Block 1890

These are the ruins of the Worthington, Scholl, and Roper Blocks—located on the north end of Merchants' Row—after the fire that occurred on June 9, 1890. The next building to the north was the Deming-Willard House, which was located at the head of Broadway and then owned by the Felton family. This house was saved thanks to the heroic efforts of the Hayward Volunteer Fire Company and others.

This photograph shows Main Street, also known as Merchants' Row, between the 1890 and 1898 fires. The building at farthest left is the Avery Block; next to it is the Kellogg and Foote Block, followed by the Adams Block and the Worthington Block. On the far right are the Scholl and Roper Blocks. All these buildings were destroyed in the 1890 fire and had been rebuilt, as shown in this image. Please note that the Worthington Block was originally constructed as a three-story building, but after the 1890 fire, it was rebuilt with two stories. Signs reading "The Colchester Advocate," "W.B. Otis," and "J.N. Adams" were on the facades of the rebuilt Kellogg and Foote and Adams Blocks just as before the 1890 fire. The *Colchester Advocate* newspaper went out of business in 1893, so this photograph must date to between 1891 and 1893.

This photograph shows the Worthington Block at 20 Main Street after it was rebuilt as a two-story structure after the June 9, 1890, Merchants' Row fire. On the left side of the first floor was the F.A. Smith Grocery Store, and the store on the right was the Haydecker Bakery. The owner of the bakery, George Haydecker, is standing on the left in the doorway of his shop. Haydecker is known to have left Colchester sometime in 1892, so this photograph must date to 1891 or 1892. At this time, the second floor of this building was occupied by Mary Whitting, a widow who ran a millinery business there. The Colchester Library Association also occupied the second floor of the Worthington Block at that time—as they had before the fire—but, unfortunately, with far fewer books. The exterior of the Worthington Block as it appears today has not changed much from what is visible here.

The last of the big Merchants' Row fires happened on May 7, 1898. The Worthington, Scholl, and Roper Blocks survived this fire, but all of the buildings from the Adams Block south to the Strong Block, plus two houses beyond (including that of Ardelia Cragin), were destroyed. In the foreground of this photograph, the Colchester Savings Bank safe is visible amongst the ruins of the Adams Block.

Joseph N. Adams (1827–1906) was the owner of the Adams Block on Merchants' Row. He was also an officer of the Colchester Savings Bank that was housed in his building. This photograph shows Adams holding a cat and standing next to the bank's safe in the ruins of his building after the 1898 Merchants' Row fire.

This photograph was taken from within the town green looking westward through the bare trees of winter toward Merchants' Row. The three buildings to the right—the Worthington, Scholl, and Roper Blocks—survived the 1898 Merchants' Row fire. However, the other buildings did not survive and had been rebuilt by the time this photograph was taken. There are several things worth noting here. First, the Adams Block, adjacent to the Worthington Block, was rebuilt as a one-story building instead of two stories, as it was before the fire. Second, the last building to the left is the Pierce Block, which had been rebuilt as a combined structure from the remains of the Strong, Pierce, and Avery Blocks. The vacant area at far left is where two houses had stood before the fire, including one belonging to the widow Ardelia Cragin, who bought the house on the corner of Broadway and Lebanon Avenue after the fire.

In 1911, another fire hit Merchants' Row; however, this time, only the Kellogg and Foote Block was destroyed. The other buildings on Main Street were saved due to the diligent actions of the Hayward Volunteer Fire Company, members of which are shown fighting the fire. Also, note the men trying to save inventory from the adjacent Pierce Block by removing it in case that building burned as well.

This photograph was taken soon after the fire of 1911 that destroyed the Kellogg and Foote Block, the ruins of which are visible in the background. The intact building beside the ruins is the Pierce Block, and the inventory that was removed from it during the fire can be seen on the town green in the foreground.

POST OFFICE BUILDING, Colchester, Conn.

The Kellogg and Foote Block, located at 36 Main Street on Merchants' Row, was rebuilt as a single-story building after the 1911 fire (instead of two stories, as it had formerly contained). The Colchester branch of the US Post Office had been located in the Kellogg and Foote building since 1886. The post office had moved back into the building after it was destroyed and rebuilt following both the 1890 and 1898 fires, and it did so again after the 1911 fire. The post office was located in the middle of the new building, with the grocery store of John Condren on the south side and the tailor shop of Hyman Buslowitz on the north side. In 1922, Joseph Agranovitch purchased the building and opened Agranovitch Hardware Store in the northern part, so this photograph predates that year. In 1931, the First National chain replaced the grocery store in the southern portion of the building. Today, this building houses a restaurant and a nail salon.

Around 1924, the Adams Block was either torn down or burned down and was not rebuilt. For a time, its former location on Merchants' Row was vacant. However, by 1927, the Harry's Place building had been moved from its original location on South Main Street to this location, as shown in this photograph. Around 1930, the Harry's Place building was moved to its current location on Broadway.

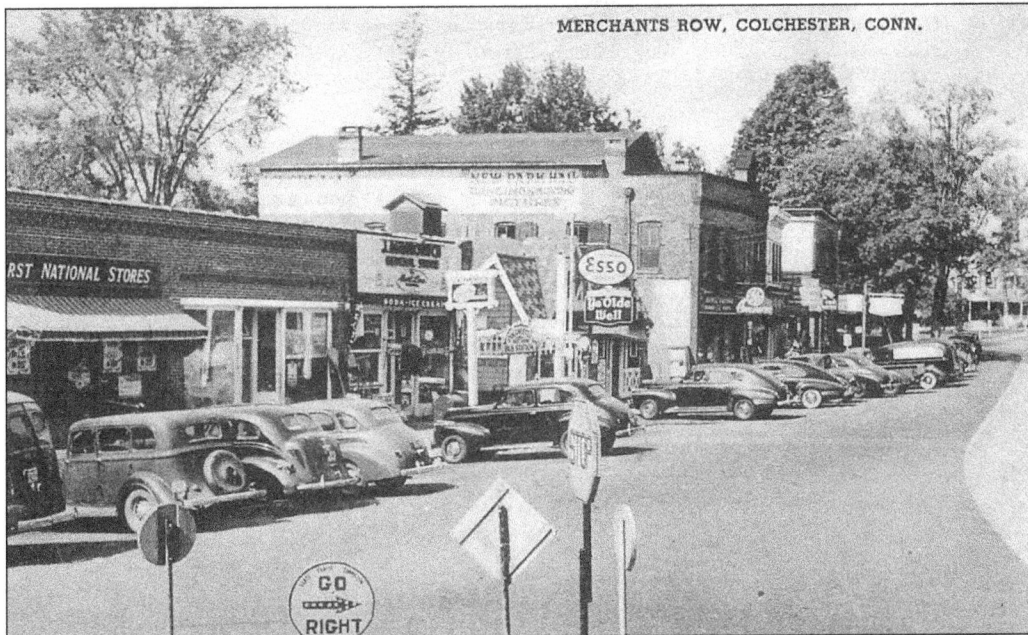

In the early 1930s, the old Adams Block site on Merchants' Row was again vacant, but by 1933, the Ye Olde Well restaurant had been built there. This restaurant operated until 1956, when it became the Colchester Inn (not to be confused with the earlier Colchester Inn hotel on South Main Street). The building burned down sometime in the 1970s, and the site has been a parking lot ever since.

This c. 1949 photograph shows the Pierce Block at 44–48 Main Street on Merchants' Row. The signs visible from left to right are for Gurian Drugs, Central Drug Co., a package store, and—in the space between the Pierce Block and the adjacent Kellogg and Foote Block—the tiny Todd's Gift Box store. Today, this building houses a massage parlor and concession shops.

This photograph shows Merchants' Row as it appeared in the 1940s. From left to right are the Kellogg and Foote Block (housing the First National Store), the Ye Olde Well restaurant, the Worthington Block (housing an appliance store, among others), the Scholl Block (housing Gregory's Soda Fountain) at 16 Main Street, and the Roper Block at 12 Main Street.

This is the earliest known photograph of the Colchester town green. The fence surrounding the green in this image is known to have been removed in 1881 and never replaced; therefore, the photograph must date to before that year. The picture was taken from the vicinity of the corner of South Main Street and Norwich Avenue, looking north, with Main Street visible in the background on the left side of the image. Note the lack of tall trees on the town green except for those in the area around its western edge. This was because the green had been laid out and landscaped in 1851, less than 30 years before this photograph was taken. As a result, one can easily see the buildings surrounding the green, including the Hayward House on Hayward Avenue (at far right).

Park, Colchester, Conn.

This postcard image looks north and shows the west side of the town green with the park's main pathway running through it. The northern half of Main Street is visible opposite the green on the left side of the image. This postcard was postmarked 1908; therefore, the photograph must date to earlier than or around that year.

PARK SCENE, COLCHESTER, CONN.

The view in this postcard image shows the town green from the corner of Hayward and Lebanon Avenues and features the northern end of the green. The street running down the left side of the image is Hayward Avenue, with Lebanon Avenue in the foreground and Main Street on the right. This photograph dates to 1916 or earlier, as the postcard was postmarked that year.

The Soldiers' Monument on the town green was dedicated on October 7, 1875. The monument is made of granite and includes a statue of a Union soldier. The monument is inscribed with the names of over 40 Colchester men "who Fell in the War for the Union 1861–5." Note the cannons around the monument's base; they were removed during World War II. The photograph probably dates to well before then.

This image of the town green shows the original gazebo, also known as the bandstand, that was built sometime in the late 1920s. This gazebo was rebuilt in the 1990s, when the wood foundation and framing were replaced with a concrete foundation and wrought-iron framing that are currently still in place.

This view of South Main Street from the town green shows the following buildings, from right to left: the Colchester Congregational Church, chapel, Bacon Academy, firehouse, C.H. Roger Store, and Lamb-Morgan House. This is perhaps the oldest known photograph of Colchester. It dates to before 1871, because the clock that was installed in the church's steeple then is not present here. As previously mentioned, the town was originally started in the area where the recreation complex and Chanticlair Golf Course are now. However, around 1714, possibly because of an inadequate water supply, the center of town was moved a mile south to this area. Around this time, the Colchester Burying Ground was laid out on the other side of these buildings. The last element of the town center as it is today was put in place in the 19th century, when the land that is now the green became public, as described in the introduction to this chapter. See chapter two for more information about the buildings shown here.

Gates' Hall

Morgan

The above photograph shows the west side of South Main Street around the turn of the 20th century, with Gates Hall on the left and the Lamb-Morgan House on the right. Gates Hall is named after brothers Hubert and Edward Gates, who built the structure in 1867. The first floor of the building housed a dry goods store for decades. The second floor had an auditorium with a stage and was the largest such space in Colchester at the time. The below photograph shows Gates Hall in the 1920s, when the A&P grocery chain moved into the first floor (where it remained for the rest of the building's existence) and the second floor became the Tip-Top Theater and Dance Hall. Gates Hall and the Lamb-Morgan House were both torn down in 1964 to make way for the expansion of an automotive business.

The above photograph shows two buildings on the west side of South Main Street. The one on the right housed the P.A. Dawley furniture store, as noted on the sign in the window. In the 1950s, this building housed the Colchester Department Store, but around 1964, it was vacated and torn down. The building on the left (and in the below photograph) is still standing at 144 South Main Street. It was built by John Kellogg around 1840. In 1863, it was purchased by Samuel Tilden. At the time the below photograph was taken, around 1890, the house was owned by Henry Morgan; therefore, it is sometimes referred to as the Tilden-Morgan House. In 1954, the building was converted into a funeral home, which it has been ever since.

BAPTIST CHURCH.   COLCHESTER, CONN.

The house at 156 South Main Street (on the right in the above photograph) was built in the 1840s. It was purchased in 1850 by Dr. Solomon Swift and was both his family home and his office. The building currently houses a law office. The building on the left is the Colchester Baptist Church constructed in 1836 and still standing at 168 South Main Street. In 1949, the Baptists merged with the Congregationalists down the street and sold this building, which has been used as an antiques shop since. The photograph at right shows Dr. Solomon Swift (1819–1895). He received his medical degree from the University of New York in 1845 and practiced medicine in Colchester for nearly 50 years, although early on, he also practiced dentistry. He served as the president of the Colchester Library Association for 26 years.

DR. SWIFT, M.D.

The house at 176 South Main Street, just to the south of the Baptist church in this photograph, was built around 1840 by Shubal Smith, who was a deacon in the church and also an attorney. This photograph dates to before 1903. In 1912, the house was purchased by John Condren and is therefore known as the Smith-Condren House.

The house at 184 South Main Street was also built around 1840 and in a style similar to that of its neighbors. The house was originally built for William Niles, and his descendants lived there for over 50 years. In 1923, the house was purchased by Evelyn Van Cleve, who owned it until her death around 1946; therefore, the house is known as the Niles–Van Cleve House.

The house at 196 South Main Street (above) was built in the 1860s by Bradford Sparrow and has a unique Stick-style front porch. Sparrow died in 1874, and the house was sold to Alden Baker, who owned it for nearly 50 years. Baker's daughter Lillian inherited the house; she was married to Edward Bunyan, so the house is known as the Sparrow-Baker-Bunyan House. The below photograph shows Lillian and Edward Bunyan in the sleigh along with their daughter Margaret. The boy holding the sled next to the horse is their son Alden. The house in the background is the Retta Buell House, which was across the street from the Bunyans' house.

In 1777, John Breed bought the property on the west side of Towne Street where this house still stands at what is now 208 South Main Street. The building was originally erected as a tavern and is known as Breed's Tavern to this day. The third floor of the structure included a large ballroom that extended the entire width of the building. Breed died in 1803, but his widow, Lucy, continued to operate the tavern until her death in 1821. In the 1790s, the tavern housed Colchester's first post office, and from 1789 to 1801, the Wooster Lodge of Masons held their meetings at the tavern. After Lucy Breed died, the building was sold to Elisha Avery, who converted it into a house. The Avery family owned this house until well into the 20th century; therefore, the house is sometimes also referred to as the Avery House.

This house at 228 South Main Street was built in the 1840s. It was sold to the First Ecclesiastical Society of Colchester in 1889 and was used as the parsonage for the Colchester Congregational Church until 1949, when it was sold to the Bochain family. This photograph was taken in 1898.

The house at 232 South Main Street is another 1840s-era house. In 1847, Erastus Standish, a local sash and blind manufacturer, bought the house. His factory was on Mill Street next to the Hayward Rubber Company complex. Erastus's son Eugene, who was the superintendent of the Hayward Rubber Company's box factory, also lived here. The photograph is dated 1924.

This house no longer exists. It was known as the Cone House because it was owned by Salmon Cone, who served as the third minister of the Colchester Congregational Church from 1792 until his death in 1830. The house burned down in the 1930s, and by 1935, a movie theater had been built on the site. In 1980, the former movie theater was sold and became the Wooster Lodge Masonic Temple building.

The house at 268 South Main Street was built in the 1840s. The front windows have distinctive decorative treatments. William B. Otis, the owner of the W.B. Otis store in the Kellogg and Foote Block on Merchants' Row, acquired this structure in 1873 and owned it until 1905; therefore, it is known as the William Otis House.

William B. Otis (1841–1914) lived in the house at what is now 268 South Main Street. He owned and operated a general store in the Kellogg and Foote Block of Merchants' Row, starting as early as 1862 and continuing as late as the 1890s. His business was quite prosperous, but he had to start over twice after the Merchants' Row fires of 1882 and 1890.

The house at 276 South Main Street was built around 1881 by George Elderkin. By that time, the popular architectural style had changed from Greek Revival to Italianate, which is reflected in the design of this house. The house remained in the Elderkin family for 70 years—until 1951—and is therefore known as the Elderkin House.

This is a view of South Main Street looking north toward the town green. The building on the east side of South Main Street (on the corner with Norwich Avenue) is the W.S. Curtis Store, which no longer exists. Note that the unpaved South Main Street is much wider than the current paved street; this was to allow room to maneuver vehicles around the ruts and potholes in the dirt road.

This photograph shows Chapman's Garage on the east side of the corner of Norwich Avenue and South Main Street, where the W.S. Curtis Store once stood. In 1920, the Harry's Place food stand was built onto the southern end of the garage, so this photograph must date to before then. Nothing further is known about Chapman's Garage. An auto parts store now occupies the site.

This c. 1919 photograph shows the east side of South Main Street. The house at right is the Bigelow House purchased by sisters Elizabeth and Sarah Bigelow in 1898. The area to the left of the house is the sisters' large garden that, in the 19th century, had been occupied by a hotel. The house and garden were razed around 1958 to make way for a commercial development.

Elizabeth Bigelow was locally famous for holding an annual shawl party in her elaborate garden next to her house on South Main Street. The side and back of the Methodist church on Norwich Avenue is clearly visible in the background of this photograph. The church was torn down in 1920, so this picture must date to before then.

The house at far left in this photograph is the Bigelow House. The small tree in the center of the image is an immature ginkgo biloba—a species that is native to China, not the United States. It is thought that this tree was a gift to the Bigelow sisters in 1898 from a relative who traveled widely in Asia. Although the house and garden are gone, the ginkgo tree still stands.

The building known as the Peters-Wickwire House was built around 1805 by Samuel Peters, who served Colchester in a number of capacities, including as its first postmaster (starting in 1799) and as a state representative for multiple terms. Addie Wickwire owned the house from 1926 to 1946. This house was torn down around 1958 for the same reason as the Bigelow House next door.

The Strong-Pendleton House, located on the east side of South Main Street, is thought to have been built around 1776. Phineas Strong was an undertaker and furniture seller in Colchester. He acquired the house in 1868, and it was in his family until 1920, when Dr. Cyrus Pendleton purchased it. Dr. Pendleton served Colchester for many years as a physician, medical examiner, treasurer, and town clerk. As town clerk, he had access to the town's old records, and he used them to write many authoritative articles about Colchester's history. The below photograph shows the fireplace that was under a staircase in the house. Dr. Pendleton died in 1950, but the house remained in his family until the 1980s. In 1986, the house was gutted, and the house's shell was moved to Hamburg Cove in Lyme, Connecticut.

The house at 147 South Main Street, known as the Chapman-Gillett House, was built in the 1830s. It was purchased by Leander Chapman in 1870 soon after he was elected warden (mayor) of Colchester for the first time. He served several more terms as warden until his death in 1905. He was also a director of the Colchester Railroad Company.

The house at 151 South Main Street (at far left in this image) was built in the 1840s and is known as the Strong-Wallack House. It has been extensively altered and no longer looks the way that it appears here. The middle house, built in 1842, still stands at 159 South Main Street and is known as the Adams House.

The house at 163 South Main Street was built around 1826. In 1879, the house was purchased by Dr. Seth Chase, who practiced medicine in Colchester for many years. After Dr. Chase died in 1891, his widow sold the house to Charles H. Dawley, the son and partner of Peleg A. Dawley, who owned a furniture store on the west side of South Main Street.

Dr. Seth Chase (1830–1891) graduated from Bacon Academy and obtained his medical degree from the College of Physicians and Surgeons in New York City, where he was class valedictorian. He eventually came back to Colchester and practiced medicine in the area for almost 40 years. He was considered something of an eccentric due to his dress and mannerisms, but he was also greatly admired for his intellect and skill as a doctor.

Dr. Chase
C. F. McIntosh, photographer, Merchants Row, Colchester, Conn.

The house at 171 South Main Street (pictured above) was built in 1818. In 1826, it was purchased by Alfred B. Pierce, and it remained in the Pierce family for the next 88 years. The photograph at left is of Alfred B. Pierce (1803–1880). He was a furniture maker, and his manufacturing shop was on this property. He was also one of the town's first undertakers, and late in his life, he owned the Pierce Block on Merchants' Row. In addition to his business pursuits, he also—at one time or another—held just about every elected office in Colchester, including selectman, justice of probate, justice of the peace, state representative, and warden (mayor) of the Borough of Colchester.

Clark Place
nor Bac[on] A[cademy]

The house at 179 South Main Street was built and purchased in 1816 by Park Benjamin, a wealthy merchant and planter in what is now Guyana in South America. Apparently, he blamed the unhealthy climate there for the death of two of his children, so he sent his remaining four children to Colchester to attend Bacon Academy. In 1822, Benjamin and his wife moved to New Haven and gathered their children there. However, in 1824, tragedy struck when Park Benjamin and one of his sons took passage back to Guyana on a boat that was lost at sea along with all hands. In 1834, the house was bought by Joshua Clark, whose family then owned it for decades. The house is known as the Clark-Cutler House, because one of the Clark heirs was married to Hobart Cutler. In 1914, the Clark family deeded the house to the Bacon Academy Board of Trustees, and it was used for many years as the home of the preceptor (principal) of Bacon Academy.

This photograph features a unique Queen Anne "gingerbread"-style house at 187 South Main Street that was built by Harley P. Buell in 1886. The property had always been in the name of Mrs. Buell, whose given name was Loretta or "Retta," for short. She owned the house for 45 years until her death in 1931, so the house is known as the Retta Buell House.

Harley P. Buell (1851–1923) came to Colchester in 1872. He worked in W.B. Otis's store until 1876, when he started apprenticing in C.H. Rogers's drugstore on South Main Street. When Rogers retired, Buell took over the business. Buell held many offices in Colchester, including first selectman, state senator, Bacon Academy Board of Trustees member, and probate judge. He died in 1923 and is buried in Linwood Cemetery.

The house at far left in this photograph of the east side of South Main Street was built in 1814 and removed in 1987. In 1867, three unmarried sisters—Frances, Mary, and Sarah Leffingwell—purchased the house, presumably to be near their older, married sister who lived across the street. The house remained in the Leffingwell family until 1951. The house in the center, at 199 South Main Street, was built around 1832; in 1839, it was purchased by the recently widowed Mary Ann (Taintor) Hyde and became known as the Hyde House. The house on the right, at 207 South Main Street, was built around 1824 for use as a general store by Avery Morgan. Starting in 1829, it was rented out to various tenants, including Abiel Bartholomew and his family (from 1832 to 1836). Abiel's son Edward Bartholomew (1822–1858) worked as the director of the Wadsworth Atheneum Museum of Art in Hartford from 1845 to 1848 and later moved to Rome, Italy, where he became a well-regarded sculptor. The photograph is dated 1923.

The structure at 219 South Main Street was built in 1824 by Avery Morgan, who also erected his store next door at the same time. He lived in this house until he and his family moved to Hartford in 1857. In 1861, Eliphalet Adams Bulkeley became the owner of the house. Eliphalet was born and raised in Colchester and was the great-great-grandson of Rev. John Bulkeley, the first minister in Colchester. Eliphalet went on to become a lawyer in East Haddam and then Hartford, Connecticut. His real interest, however, was in life insurance, and in 1850, he founded Aetna Life Insurance Company and served as its president until his death in 1872. The house on South Main Street in Colchester was used by Eliphalet Bulkeley and his descendants as a summer house until 1923, the year this photograph is dated. The building is now home to a bank.

The house at 239 South Main Street was built around 1840 and owned by John T. Bulkeley, a brother of Eliphalet A. Bulkeley, who lived next door. In 1846, Hiram Weeks bought this house, but in 1866, John T. Bulkeley bought it back. John was a Colchester policeman for years; he died in 1882. In 1910, the house was purchased by Henry Bailey.

The house at 251 South Main Street was built around 1873. In 1880, it was sold to Charlotte Destin, who lived across the street. She rented the house to various tenants until 1897, when she sold it to William Palmer. In 1918, Rev. Byron Remington, pastor of the Colchester Baptist Church, bought the house. Since he lived in the Baptist parsonage on Linwood Avenue, he also rented this house out to tenants.

Electra (Williams) Clark purchased the property at 263 South Main Street from J.T. Bulkeley in 1879. She quickly proceeded to build the Queen Anne–style house shown in this 1923 photograph. Clark died in 1913, and her estate sold the house to Cora Carrier; therefore, the house is known as the Clark-Carrier House.

This house no longer exists. It was built in 1882 by William Wagner. In 1917, it was sold to Samuel Singer. The photograph is dated 1923. The house was torn down in the late 1980s. The site now contains a propane service company and a restaurant.

BAPTIST PARSONAGE AND LIBRARY.   COLCHESTER. CONN.

Cragin Memorial Library, at 8 Linwood Avenue, is on the right in this photograph. The library was completed in 1905 on the site of Ardelia Cragin's house, which was destroyed in the Merchants' Row fire of 1898 (see chapter two for more information about this house). The house on the left, at 24 Linwood Avenue, was built in the 1850s for the Ballard family. In 1908, the house was bequeathed to the Colchester Baptist Church and used as its parsonage until it merged with the Colchester Congregational Church across the street in 1949. In 2001, as part of a plan to expand the library and its parking area, the Town of Colchester purchased the property, renovated it, and then leased it to the Colchester Historical Society. It has been used as the society's meeting place and museum ever since.

Nothing is known about the partially visible house at far right; it no longer exists. The house next to it, at 36 Linwood Avenue, was built in the 1870s or 1880s and was owned by the Joseph Smith family for decades. The building next to 36 Linwood Avenue was owned by Smith and was a blacksmith shop that no longer exists. The house next to the blacksmith shop, at 52 Linwood Avenue, was the home of Elijah Ransom, a local merchant who had a store on Hayward Avenue.

The house at 68 Linwood Avenue was built in the 1860s to serve as the parsonage for the Colchester Methodist Episcopal congregation, which had a church located on Norwich Avenue. By 1889, it had become a privately owned house, and it has had many owners since then. The building is currently home to a financial planning business.

This is a view of Linwood Avenue looking east toward the Colchester Congregational Church, which is visible in the center background. The house at left still stands at 68 Linwood Avenue; at the time this photograph was taken, it may still have been the parsonage for the Methodist Episcopal church. Note that the house at 68 Linwood Avenue does not yet have the wraparound veranda that is now present. The house at right is unidentified and is no longer present. Where the road is shown splitting, Linwood Avenue goes to the left, with the road veering to the right corresponding to what is now the private drive between the Colchester Federated Church and Day Hall. Linwood Avenue was not paved until the 1930s, and this photograph probably dates to significantly earlier than that.

The above photograph shows the north side of Lebanon Avenue sometime before being destroyed in a fire in October 1923. The below photograph shows the same area after the fire. The building at right above and in the background below is the structure at 59 Lebanon Avenue, which now houses a pizza shop. The fire started in Joseph London's garage and quickly spread to the adjacent buildings. At that time, Colchester's Hayward Volunteer Fire Company had only its original 1854 hand pumper to fight this large fire, and it clearly was not up to the task. The arrival of a modern fire engine from a neighboring town was the only thing that saved more buildings from burning in Colchester. As a result, in 1924, the fire company was authorized to purchase its first fire truck.

The above photograph shows the home (at left) and the dry goods and grocery store (at right) of Charles H. Bailey. Both of these buildings still stand at 83 and 87 Lebanon Avenue, respectively. Charles Bailey started the store in 1866 and retired and turned over the store to his son Henry in 1891. This photograph dates to before 1891. The Bailey store building now houses an insurance agency. The Gothic-style house in the below photograph is located at 95 Lebanon Avenue and was the next building east of the Bailey store on the other side of the west end of Hammond Court; it now houses a clothing consignment store.

The above photograph shows a view of Lebanon Avenue looking east toward the Colchester Railroad passenger station and the area beyond it known as Dublin. The Colchester Railroad spur was completed in 1877 (see the chapter introduction for more information). Dublin got its name because of the Irish immigrants who lived in this area and worked in the nearby rubber factory. There were several boardinghouses nearby to accommodate the single workers. This photograph was taken in 1894 from a railroad trestle that ran over Lebanon Avenue to allow freight trains to come and go from the rubber factory across the street. The postcard image shown below is postmarked 1910 and shows the passenger station. The building still stands at 199 Lebanon Avenue and is now a package store.

R. R. Station, Colchester, Conn.

THE OLD RANSOM STORE, COLCHESTER, CONN.

The building that housed the old E. Ransom and Son Store (above) and its replacement (below) no longer exists. The site where these buildings stood was on the corner of Hayward and Lebanon Avenues and is now part of the lawn of the Ralph Isham House. In 1706, this was the site of the house that the town gave to Rev. John Bulkeley, the first minister of the Colchester Congregational Church. Around the start of the 19th century, the house was converted into a store. In 1856, Elijah Ransom opened his general store in the old and greatly altered building. In 1884, he tore down the old store and built a new one on the same site, as shown below. The new building was destroyed in a fire in 1916, and the store was never rebuilt.

Ransom's corner.
The new store

The house at 11 Hayward Avenue on the left was built in 1820 by Ralph Isham and is considered one of the finest old houses still present in Colchester. Isham, a merchant, died in 1845. The following year, his heirs sold the house to Henry Burr, who was married to one of Isham's daughters. Burr was a business partner of Nathaniel Hayward in Lisbon, Connecticut, and it is thought that it was Burr who, in 1847, convinced Hayward to build his new rubber factory on the large tract of land that Burr owned in Colchester. Burr left Colchester after his wife died in 1857, but he kept the house and rented it to various tenants. In 1883, the house and eight acres of property were sold to Charles Williams. The house remained in the Williams family until 1927. The property includes a carriage house and, at one time, had a greenhouse, an apple orchard, and a vineyard. The building now houses commercial offices.

Old Ralph Isham place

The house on the left, at 23 Hayward Avenue, is known as the Joseph Isham House and was built by Isham in 1765. Joseph Isham Jr. was a wealthy merchant who also served Colchester as a selectman from 1781 until 1805. Joseph died in 1810, but his widow continued to live in the house until her death in 1834. His son Ralph also lived in the house until he built his own place next door in 1820. In 1879, the house was purchased by Dr. Rexford Carrington and his wife, Sophia, who proceeded to make many repairs and modifications to the house, adding a dormer, cupola, and verandah. After Dr. Carrington died in 1886, Sophia operated a tearoom in the house for years; she died in 1913. The Gothic Revival–style cottage to the right, at 31 Hayward Avenue, was built by George Avery on a tiny eighth of an acre lot in 1870. The house was in the Avery family until 1912.

The house at 35 Hayward Avenue was built around 1775 by Dudley Wright, a wealthy local merchant. This house has been witness to a lot of Colchester's history, as it has been occupied by several prominent families. Dudley Wright was followed by his son-in-law Dr. John R. Watrous, whose contributions to Colchester are too numerous to mention. Dr. Watrous was followed by his son-in-law Dr. Frederick Morgan, and he was followed by the most famous resident of Colchester, Nathaniel Hayward, who was involved in the invention of vulcanized rubber. Hayward bought the house, which is now named after him, in 1848, the same year he completed his rubber factory. Hayward was a civic-minded man who, in 1850, donated his front yard to the town; it became the town green. He was also instrumental in creating the volunteer fire company that bears his name. Hayward died in 1865, but his descendants owned this house until 1940. Today, the building is home to an inn and offices.

This photograph shows the interior of the southwest room of the Hayward House at 35 Hayward Avenue. When the house was built around 1775, only the best materials and craftsmanship were used, as evidenced by the fireplace tiles and the fine wood paneling on the walls. This large and lavish house hosted many social events over the years, including receptions, balls, and parties.

The two buildings in this photograph are located at 45 and 53 Hayward Avenue. The building at left is the carriage house, and the one at right is the granary; both were part of the Hayward House estate. These Italianate-style buildings were erected between 1858 and 1868. The carriage house until recently was a restaurant. Note that the carriage house no longer has a cupola.

The adjacent houses at 55 and 63 Hayward Avenue were built in the early 1840s in a similar style. There is no known period image of the 55 Hayward Avenue house, but it probably looked like its neighbor. It was built by Daniel Brown but is referred to as the Wickwire-Bochain House after later owners. It now houses a financial planning firm. The house shown above is the one at 63 Hayward Avenue and was built by Pomeroy Hall. It was purchased in 1866 by Joseph N. Adams, who owned the Adams Block on Merchants' Row. The house remained in the Adams family until 1939. It now houses an insurance agency. The photograph at left is of Adams (1830–1906), a prominent local merchant and businessman.

This photograph was taken in 1903 from the town green looking east toward the southern end of Hayward Avenue. The house at left, located at 67 Hayward Avenue, was built by Pomeroy Hall in 1848, and he sold it to Roxy Lathrop, a widow, who owned it until she died in 1875. In 1886, William Strong bought the house, and his descendants owned it until 1946; therefore, it is known as the Lathrop-Strong House. Today, it houses a day care center. The middle building is the Calvary Episcopal Church, built in 1867 and torn down in 1920 (see chapter two for more information). The house to the right of the church on the corner of Hayward and Norwich Avenues was built around 1844 by John Schofield. Joseph Brooks bought the house in 1851, and it became known as the Brooks House. In 1902, Edward Day, whose father owned the house next door on Norwich Avenue, bought the Brooks House, and he tore it down sometime before 1914. The corner is now occupied by a bank.

The view in this photograph looks east from the town green to Norwich Avenue. The building at farthest right was the F.T. Avery Hardware store and residence at 32 Norwich Avenue. Around 1925, it was sold to the Cohen brothers, and soon after, it was partially destroyed in a fire and then rebuilt as a garment factory. Today, the front part of the building houses an ice-cream shop. The building next to 32 Norwich Avenue is the Wheeler Block at 40 Norwich Avenue. The building to the left of the Wheeler Block is the Manley Block, and it also housed a hardware store; in 1914, this building was removed in order to create a playground for the Ransom School, which was located next door in the Wheeler Block. The building at farthest left is the Colchester Methodist Episcopal Church that was built in 1843 and torn down in 1920 (see chapter two for more information).

Wheeler Block

The building at 40 Norwich Avenue was erected in 1872 by Joshua B. Wheeler and housed several different stores on the lower floors and a Masonic lodge on the top floor. It is one of the few known Second Empire–style buildings in Colchester. In 1889, Wheeler's daughter Emeline Ransom inherited the property, and in 1910, she did a remarkable thing—she sold the property to the town for $1 with the stipulation that it be used as a public school. From 1910 through 1936, the building housed grades two through four of the first school district and was called the Ransom School. After it was no longer needed to be used as a school following the opening of the Central School, it became Colchester's first town hall. In 1992, after the town hall was moved to a new building up the street, the Wheeler Block's usefulness was still not done, as it then became the Colchester Youth Center, which it still is today.

The house at 48 Norwich Avenue is the oldest surviving building in Colchester. It was completed in 1702 by Nathaniel Foote, the son of Colchester's founder. The house was originally located somewhere on Old Hebron Road and was moved in the early 19th century to the grounds of what is now 191 Broadway. In 1925, the house was donated to the Colchester chapter of the Daughters of the American Revolution (DAR) and moved a second time to its current location on Norwich Avenue. Since then, the building has been known as the DAR-Foote House. The above photograph dates to sometime after the building's second move. The house is now owned by the Bacon Academy Board of Trustees. The below photograph shows the interior of the house. The paneling is period but not original to the house.

The photograph at right shows the Wheeler House, which was on the south side of Norwich Avenue a little east of where the DAR-Foote House is today. This was the home of Joshua B. Wheeler (pictured below; 1798–1882), a prominent Colchester businessman who built the Wheeler Block just down the street. It is not known when the house was built or by whom. Wheeler died in 1882, and sometime after that, the house was converted into the Oliver Woodhouse Lodge of the Knights of Pythias fraternal organization. The building was torn down in the early 1970s. The site is now occupied by a bank.

WHEELER HOMESTEAD.

The house pictured above was built in 1847 at 63 Norwich Avenue, just east of the corner of Hayward and Norwich Avenues. In 1865, it was purchased by Erastus S. Day, whose descendants lived there for over 100 years. The house was torn down in the 1990s, and a bank is there now. The above photograph dates to before 1920. Erastus Day's ancestry goes all the way back to John Day, who settled in what is now the Westchester section of Colchester in 1702. In fact, John Day's homestead was where Day Pond State Park is now located. Erastus Day (1836–1921), pictured at left, served Colchester as a prominent lawyer, state representative, and probate judge. Remarkably, from 1897 to 1909, he served as a US consul in England.

Erastus S. Day

The above photograph shows the Colchester Grange Hall (now the Colchester Senior Center) at 95 Norwich Avenue. The building was erected around 1884 by the Colchester chapter of the Grand Army of the Republic Civil War veterans' organization. The Colchester Grange No. 78 bought the building in 1901. Around 1956, the Bacon Academy Board of Trustees purchased the building and doubled its size with a new addition, which completed the appearance of the building that still stands today. The board of trustees used the remodeled building as the Bacon Academy's arts and science department. The senior center opened in 1980. The below photograph dates to before 1920 and looks west on Norwich Avenue from the vicinity of the grange hall. The Wheeler House and the Methodist church are visible on the left.

This is the Charles T. Smith house that was on the north side of Norwich Avenue. It is not known when or by whom the house was built, but it is apparent from the photograph that it was upscale, and its garden was quite lush. This house was removed or torn down by 1990, when the new Colchester Town Hall was built in this area.

This photograph shows the large farm that straddled New London Road about a mile south of Colchester and was owned by the brothers Charles and Horace Smith. In the late 1880s, this site was considered for the relocation of the Storrs Agricultural School, but in the end, the school was not relocated and later became the University of Connecticut. This area is now occupied by a Connecticut Department of Transportation facility.

Two

INSTITUTIONS

RELIGIOUS, EDUCATIONAL, AND CIVIC

The first and most important institution in any colonial Connecticut town was the Congregational church. Rev. John Bulkeley was appointed the first minister of the Colchester Ecclesiastical Society in 1703 and served until his death in 1731. His first church was a primitive 20-by-20-foot building located near where the golf course is now. Around 1714, the town center was relocated to where it is today, and a new church was built near where the Colchester Federated Church is located.

In 1728, residents in the Westchester section of town petitioned the Connecticut General Assembly for another ecclesiastical society. In 1729, the petition was granted, and the Westchester Ecclesiastical Society built its church in 1730 on what is now Cemetery Road.

In 1771, Colchester's First Ecclesiastical Society tore down the group's old church and built a larger one designed by noted joiner Isaac Fitch. The second church was torn down in 1841 and replaced with the Greek Revival church there today. Other Colchester religious institutions will be discussed later in this chapter.

Educational institutions were also of major importance. Until 1936, Colchester had as many as 15 school districts to provide primary education to its children. Bacon Academy opened in 1803. In addition to housing a primary school, it had a curriculum that, in effect, made it the first secondary and college-preparation school in the state. Associated with the academy but separate was the School for Colored Children. Bacon Academy was integrated in 1848.

Colchester's civic institutions, such as the post office, the fire company, and the library, have also been of great importance. Nathaniel Hayward helped found the Hayward Volunteer Fire Company in 1854, and that year, the company purchased a Hunneman hand-pumped fire engine; the following year, the company built a firehouse on South Main Street to serve as a base of operations. In 1861, the Colchester Library Association (CLA), which had been organized in 1859, established its first reading room on the second floor of the firehouse.

Bacon Academy and Congregational Church, Colchester.

This print from John Warner Barber's *History and Antiquities of Every Town in Connecticut*, published in 1836, shows a view of what is now South Main Street. On the right is the Colchester Congregational Church, built in 1771, that faced what is now Linwood Avenue. This church was torn down in 1841 to make way for the current church. To the left (south) of the church is Bacon Academy. Note that the hood over the academy's front door had not yet been added and that the original open cupola/bell tower is present. Also, note that Day Hall—now between Colchester Federated Church and Bacon Academy—had not yet been built. To the left of Bacon Academy is the church's first conference house. In the 1850s, when the church no longer needed this building, it was sold to C.H. Rogers, who converted it into a drugstore. Just visible in the trees to the right of the church is the School for Colored Children.

CONGREGATIONAL CHURCH AND CHAPEL, COLCHESTER, CONN.

The Colchester Congregational Church at 60 South Main Street was built in 1841. Around 1885, the church was remodeled with changes that are shown in this c. 1910 postcard image, including the colored-glass windows and the finials added to the top of the steeple. By the time of the church's next major renovation in 1929, these changes were considered outdated and thus reversed. To the left is the church's second conference house, later referred to as "the chapel." This Italianate building at 80 South Main Street was constructed in 1858. The church's 1929 renovations were paid for by Edward M. Day, and in gratitude, the church gave him this building, which he also paid to have renovated. He then gave it to the Bacon Academy Board of Trustees, who renamed the building Day Hall in Day's honor. The academy used the building as a badly needed auditorium and for additional classroom space. It now houses a nursery school.

The Colchester Congregational Church's interior was extensively renovated around 1885 to give it a more elaborate Victorian look, which was popular at the time. The remodeling included the installation of colored-glass windows, an upgrade of the ceiling and wall decorations, and the conversion of the pews to a semi-circular configuration. The photograph at left shows the interior of the church looking toward the front of the church, and the below photograph shows the view toward the rear of the church. The pipe organ in the balcony was donated to the church in 1871. By 1929, the 1885 changes to the church were considered out of fashion, and it was renovated again with straight pews and less-ornate details to restore the more original Colonial look that it still has today. Both of these photographs date to the late 1880s.

The above photograph is of the current Westchester Congregational Church at 98 Cemetery Road in the Westchester section of Colchester. This church—the society's third in this location—was built in 1848 after the second church burned down in a fire the previous year. This church, as well as the Colchester Congregational Church and the former Colchester Baptist Church, were built within a span of 12 years and were all designed in a Greek Revival style that was popular at the time. The undated postcard below shows the minimalistic style of the interior of this church.

WESTCHESTER, CONN.

WESTCHESTER CONGREGATIONAL CHURCH

The Colchester Baptist Church at 168 South Main Street was built in 1836. Note the presence of two front entry doors with a large arched window between them. Unlike the Colchester and Westchester Congregational Churches, which were built a few years later, the Baptist church had a spire on top of its steeple. The steeple and spire were destroyed by the hurricane of 1938, which did so much damage in Connecticut. In 1949, the Baptists merged with the Colchester Congregational Church, thus forming the Colchester Federated Church of today. The Baptist church building was purchased by Nathan and Israel Liverant and converted into an antiques shop that is still there. The undated photograph below shows the interior of the church. The interior space of the building is still much the same as it was then—minus the pews and altar.

Starting in the early 1800s, a Methodist circuit preacher would periodically come to Colchester and be invited to preach in a local home. This practice continued until an official congregation was formed, and in 1843, a Methodist Episcopal church was built on Norwich Avenue, as shown above. This church was in use until it the congregation was disbanded in 1915. The church was torn down in either 1919 or 1920. The undated photograph at right shows the interior of the church. At some point, Edward M. Day bought the property, and in 1925, he gave it to the Colchester chapter of the Daughters of the American Revolution so they could move the DAR-Foote House, which had just been given to them, to this site, where it remains.

The Calvary Episcopal Church was organized in 1865, and the church building opened for services in 1867. There were only three resident rectors of this church, with the last either resigning or retiring in 1880. After that, the church combined with St Peter's Episcopal Church in Hebron, and that church's rectors conducted services in the Colchester church each Sunday afternoon and in the morning on the third Sunday of the month. The congregation disbanded sometime in the 1910s, and the church was torn down in 1920. The below photograph shows the interior of the church and looks toward the altar area in the rear of the building.

At right in this photograph is the original St. Andrew Roman Catholic Church building, which was completed in 1855 but not dedicated until 1865. At left is the second church rectory, which was completed around 1883. The area where these buildings were located is called Dublin because of the Irish immigrants who settled in this part of Colchester to work in the nearby rubber factory that operated from 1848 to 1893. In 1874, the parish built a parochial school that later became a public school; it no longer exists. The church served the local Catholic population until 1962, when a new parish center opened on Norwich Avenue. In 1967, the current St. Andrew Church and rectory buildings also opened there. The old rectory and church buildings were converted into apartments and still stand at 47 and 51 Windham Avenue, respectively.

The photograph shows the Congregation Ahavath Achim Synagogue on Lebanon Avenue shortly after it was built in 1913. This was the second synagogue in Colchester, but it was the first constructed with the intention of being a synagogue. The first synagogue was a house on Windham Avenue that was converted into a synagogue in 1902. There were a few Jewish people living in Colchester before the sudden closing of the Colchester Rubber Company in 1893. However, after the company closed, the Jewish population grew considerably over the following decades. This was due, in part, to various Jewish aid agencies promoting Colchester for the resettlement of Jewish people, primarily from New York City. Colchester was an attractive location because for a long time after the closing of the rubber plant, inexpensive land and buildings were available. These Jewish settlers not only established successful farms but also businesses of many kinds that helped Colchester to recover economically after the rubber plant closed. In 1960, the old synagogue was torn down, and a new one was built nearby and is still serving the community today.

This photograph of Bacon Academy, located at 84 Main Street, dates to around 1900. Pierpoint and Abigail (Newton) Bacon were the wealthiest couple in Colchester when they died in 1800. Pierpoint Bacon bequeathed his entire estate to Colchester to be used for the construction of a new school. A state charter granted in 1801 established a board of trustees to oversee the school, and the board decided that it should provide secondary and college preparation—as well as primary—education, all free to Colchester residents. Starting in 1842, the higher education classes were opened to females, and in 1848, Bacon Academy was integrated. Note the presence of the hood over the door, shutters on the windows, and a balustrade and a closed cupola on the roof. These were all additions made to the building in 1856, and the hood and closed cupola are still in place. The last class graduated from the old school in 1962, when a new Bacon Academy High School opened. This building is now used for the town's alternative education program.

Unionville School House

The above photograph features Colchester District School No. 3 on Miller Road near the junction with Old Hartford Road. This school was also referred to as the Unionville School. This school is typical of one-room district schoolhouses in Colchester in the late 19th and early 20th centuries. It is not known when this photograph was taken. The below photograph shows the interior of the District No. 3 School with a class in session, and it is dated 1912–1913. This building was in operation until November 1936, when the new Central School opened and Colchester's primary school students were transported there and all the district schools shut down except the Westchester schools. It is not known what happened to this building.

This 1922 photograph shows Colchester District School No. 9 on McDonald Road north of Marvin Road; this school was also referred to as the Marvin School. This school is typical of the one-room district schoolhouses in Colchester in the late 19th and early 20th centuries. This building was either removed or torn down sometime after 1936.

Pictured here is Mary Shea's 1924 third-grade class at the Ransom School in the Wheeler Block at 40 Norwich Avenue. From 1911 to 1936, the First District School students in grades two through four were housed in the Wheeler Block instead of in old Bacon Academy, presumably because of overcrowding.

This photograph shows the Westchester Northwest District School that was on the west side of Bull Hill Road next to Bull Hill Cemetery. It is not known when this building was constructed, but it appears to be more upscale than the District Schools No. 3 and 9 shown on the previous two pages. This building's fate is unknown; however, around 1900, a smaller, less-elegant schoolhouse was erected on this site. Both structures are now gone.

This photograph shows the Westchester Northeast District School that was on the north side of River Road. It is not known when this building was erected. The photograph dates to sometime in the 1920s, judging from the children's clothing. It is not known when the building was removed or torn down, but it was still in operation as late as 1956.

The Central School on Norwich Avenue opened in November 1936. The opening of this school marked the end of the Colchester district schools (except those in Westchester), as from then on, Colchester's public elementary school students were transported here. This school was substantially enlarged in the 1950s, and in the following decades, it has been greatly altered via demolition, rebuilding, and remodeling.

The top portion of this early 1940s photograph shows the Central School on Norwich Avenue, looking west. The lower portion of the image shows Mrs. Shea's 1943 third-grade class posed in front of the school. Later, the school became the Central Middle School. In 1990, it was renamed William J. Johnston Middle School after a local Congressional Medal of Honor winner who had recently died.

POST OFFICE BLOCK, Colchester, Conn.

The Colchester branch of the US Post Office was established in 1799, when Samuel A. Peters was appointed Colchester's first postmaster. Peters probably kept the post office where he lived, which was the building known both then and now as Breed's Tavern, located at 208 South Main Street. Peters served as postmaster for 19 years. The other long-serving postmaster in the 19th century was Charles H. Rogers, who served for 24 years from 1861 to 1885 and kept the post office in his store on South Main Street. During the post office's first 100-plus years, when a new postmaster was appointed, the post office location would usually also change. Giles Wickwire succeeded Rogers as postmaster in 1885, and the post office was moved to Merchants' Row, where it stayed until 1940, despite changes of postmasters. This photograph of the Kellogg and Foote Block, with the post office in the center section, dates to the 1920s. By 1952, the post office was in its current location at 103 South Main Street.

C. F. McIntosh   R. R. 3   1905

In the late 19th century, in order to get mail in a small town like Colchester, a person had to go to the post office and pick it up. Starting in 1901, Colchester became part of the US Postal Service's Rural Free Delivery (RFD) system. At first, there was only one route, but by 1904, there were four routes. In order to receive this service, one had to put up an approved mailbox. Parcel delivery was added to the service in 1911, and by 1930, the modern mail and package service was in place. This 1905 photograph shows Cortis. F. McIntosh (1851–1923) beside his RFD route No. 3 horse and buggy. He manned this route from its start in 1902 until 1922, the year before he died. From 1879 to 1890, he was a professional photographer in the area and had studios in Moodus, Chester, and Colchester. Notably, McIntosh is the person who took a number of the photographs in this book from that period.

On February 6, 1854, the Borough of Colchester voted to authorize the creation of the Hayward Volunteer Fire Company, the purchase of a fire engine and other equipment, and the digging of rainwater cisterns. The 1854 Hunneman hand pumper shown in this photograph was purchased that October, and the following year, a firehouse/headquarters was built on South Main Street. The photograph dates to the early 1900s.

This c. 1931 image shows the Hayward Fire Company firehouse and headquarters at 100 South Main Street. The company's first fire truck, a 1924 REO, is in front of the firehouse. Around the time this picture was taken, the firehouse still had its original single-bay configuration. The firehouse is now home to the Colchester Hayward Fire Museum and displays the original 1854 Hunneman hand pumper.

The Colchester Library Association (CLA) was formed in 1859 following the merger of the male-only Library Association of Colchester and the Ladies Library Association. In 1861, the CLA got its first reading room when it occupied the second floor of the firehouse at 100 South Main Street. In 1879, the state legislature granted the association a charter of incorporation. In 1886, the library moved into the second floor of the Worthington Block on Merchants' Row. The fire of 1890 completely destroyed the library and its contents. After the Worthington Block was rebuilt, the CLA moved back into the building, albeit with a greatly reduced collection. The CLA survived the Merchants' Row fire of 1898, but the house of Dr. Edwin B. Cragin's mother on Linwood Avenue did not. In 1903, Dr. Cragin donated the empty site and the money to build and stock a library, which was dedicated in 1905 and named Cragin Memorial Library in honor of Dr. Cragin's late father; this photograph dates to around that time.

Colchester Library Association in Worthington Block.

The above photograph shows the Colchester Library Association's main reading room on the second floor of the Worthington Block on Merchants' Row between 1886 and 1890. The below photograph is of the reading room's annex. As is clearly visible in these two photographs, the association's collections numbered in the thousands at this time. Unfortunately, except for what was out in circulation, this collection was completely destroyed in the Merchants' Row fire of 1890. When the association moved into the rebuilt Worthington Block, they had to start their collection again from nearly nothing. The association operated out of the new Worthington Block until Cragin Memorial Library was built on nearby Linwood Avenue and opened in 1905.

Three

BUSINESSES

HOSPITALITY, RETAIL, AND INDUSTRIAL

Businesses are an important part of any community. Because Colchester is located on the roads between Hartford and New London and Middletown and Willimantic, hospitality businesses, such as taverns and inns, appeared early in the town's existence. In the second half of the 19th century, when the rubber factory was going strong, there was a major hotel on South Main Street. In the first half of the 20th century, Colchester had a robust resort business, with several hotels primarily catering to a Jewish clientele, which often caused Colchester's population to double during the summer months. At this time, Colchester became known as "the Catskills of Connecticut."

Retail stores were also important to the community. From the beginning, there were general stores that sold dry goods, groceries, and toiletries, often by barter. In the 19th century, the Colchester business community expanded to include drugstores, furniture stores, jewelry stores, clothing stores, and more. The portion of Main Street across from the town green evolved into a commercial hub and came to be known as Merchants' Row.

Early on, the main industrial business in Colchester, besides farming, was the operation of various types of water-powered mills. These mills sawed lumber and ground grain, among other things. With the exception of the C.H. Norton Company paper mill, these mills were all gone by the early 20th century. Colchester was home to a business of national importance called the Hayward Rubber Company that made various footwear products from vulcanized rubber. In 1887, the company was sold and renamed the Colchester Rubber Company. There was also a canning factory, a wheel company, and a creamery in town at various times.

In the late 19th and early 20th centuries, Colchester had a variety of service businesses. These included medical, dental, and legal practices; funeral parlors; and blacksmith shops. During this time, Colchester even had its own bank and newspaper. (Because photographs of some of these businesses have been shown in previous chapters, no photographs of service businesses will be included in this one.)

KEENEY HOUSE, COLCHESTER, CONN.

The South Main Street location where the post office is now located was home to a tavern or hotel for over a century. Starting in the late 1700s, the house on this site included a tavern. In 1856, Albert Keeney bought the building and expanded it into a hotel, as shown in the above image of an advertisement for the Keeney House. In 1867, it became the Howard House. In 1876, Simon Hooker bought the property, and soon after, the building burned down. The below photograph shows the new hotel that was built on the site and, until 1886, was called the Hooker House. By 1894, the hotel had become the Colchester Inn, which only lasted a short time before a fire destroyed it. Around 1903, Elizabeth and Sarah Bigelow bought the now-vacant lot and turned it into a large garden that was greatly admired.

The Dembers Hotel   Colchester, Conn.

In 1911, Barnett Dember bought the property at 156 Halls Hill Road and built the hotel shown here. Dember was one of the Jewish people who arrived in the years after the rubber factory closed and Colchester's economy had crashed. The Dember Elmwood House catered to a mostly Jewish clientele and operated until the Great Depression did it in around 1933. There were several others like it in Colchester at that time.

LEVY'S GRAND VIEW and LAKE COLCHESTER, CONN.

The largest resort in Colchester's history was the Grand View House on Linwood Cemetery Road. Charles Levy bought the 100-acre property in 1922 and quickly built a multiple-building complex next to a small lake, as shown in this picture. The resort operated as Grand View House into the 1950s. In 1961, it was sold and became the Lincoln Lake Lodge. It is now private property.

BROADWAY HOUSE, COLCHESTER, CONN.

The Broadway House Hotel and annex present another example of the hospitality businesses that flourished during Colchester's "Catskills of Connecticut" days in the first half of the 20th century. The main hotel shown in the above photograph was built by Abraham and Rose Jaffe around 1920; it no longer exists. It was located back from Broadway on what is now Jaffe Terrace. The Broadway House annex building shown in the below photograph was previously the Jaffe Overlook Hotel and still exists as apartments at 116 Broadway, just north of Harry's Place.

BROADWAY HOUSE (ANNEX) COLCHESTER, CONN.

Harry's Place, a popular drive-in restaurant located at 104 Broadway, is known throughout Connecticut. It was started in 1920 by Harry Schmuckler and was first located on the east side of South Main Street and attached to Chapman's Garage on the corner of Norwich Avenue, as shown here.

TOWN GREEN AND MERCHANTS ROW

Around 1927, the Harry's Place building was moved from South Main Street to the vacant lot on Merchants' Row where the Adams Block had been, as shown in this photograph. The building was in this location until around 1930, when it was moved to its current location on Broadway. In the 1930s, Rubin "Ruby" Cohen, who had worked for Harry Schmuckler, bought the restaurant; Cohen owned it until 1978.

The building in the above photograph was on South Main Street next to the firehouse. It was constructed in the 1830s as the conference house for the Colchester Congregational Church just down the street. In 1853, it was sold to Charles H. Rogers, who converted it into a drugstore. In 1876, Rogers took on H.P. Buell as an apprentice, and Buell eventually took over the business, but as shown, Buell kept the C.H. Rogers sign on the building along with his own. In 1889, this building burned to the ground, and the new store (shown below) was built on the site in 1890. The sign in the window on the left side of the building is for William Daudey's jewelry shop. This structure later became home to the Earl Holmes Drug Store.

By 1917, H.P. Buell had taken on Earl R. Holmes as his apprentice in his drugstore on South Main Street next to the firehouse. Holmes took over the business after Buell's death in 1923 and operated the store until 1960; thus, there was a drugstore on this site for over a century. The above photograph of the Holmes store dates to the 1940s. The below photograph shows the interior of the Holmes Drug Store. The sign in the middle foreground reads "Kodak," and the sign on the far left reads "Kibbe chocolates." After Holmes closed his store, the building housed a pizza restaurant for a time. In 1980, the long, empty building was torn down. Today, a reproduction of the School for Colored Children occupies part of the site.

Earl R. Holmes (1894–1977) was a lifelong resident of Colchester. He owned and operated the Holmes Drug Store on South Main Street. In addition to being a shop owner, he was also a prolific amateur photographer, and while most of his photographs are not credited, there is little doubt that some of the photographs in this book were taken by him. He also liked to make home movies, many of which are now in possession of the Colchester Historical Society and are occasionally shown at society events. He was also an avid ham radio operator and was often the first in town to hear of world events. After he closed his store in 1960, he worked as a mailman for many years.

This photograph is of the L.C. and C.F. Brown Store in the Gates Hall building on the west side of South Main Street, where a defunct automobile dealership now stands. The C.F. Brown Store opened in 1884, and it dealt in dry goods, groceries, and grain. It is not known when the store went out of business. The building was torn down in 1964.

The building at left is Samuel Stern's general store at 203 Lebanon Avenue, next to the railroad passenger station. Stern was a Russian Jewish immigrant who made good in Colchester. In the 19th century, this building was a boardinghouse for the rubber company. This image is from a postcard that was postmarked 1919, so the photograph must date to that year or earlier.

Pictured here around 1915 is the general store of Joseph Agranovitch on Norwich Avenue, next to the Wheeler Block. The store was started by Joseph's father, Isador Agranovitch, who emigrated from Russia with his family in 1890 and settled in Colchester in 1905. This is one example of the many Jewish families who moved to Colchester around this time and became successful in various occupations.

This c. 1933 photograph shows Skawinski's Filling Station on Broadway, at the corner of Amston Road. The people shown here are the owner of the station, Stephen Skawinski, and his son Leon. Stephen Skawinski represents another wave of immigration to Colchester from Eastern Europe, but this group was of the Catholic faith rather than Jewish.

This photograph shows the Boot and Shoe Building on Mill Street that was part of the Hayward Rubber Company factory complex between Lebanon and Norwich Avenues. This building is where mostly female workers assembled the parts, made elsewhere in the factory, into the final shoe and boot products ready for finishing. After being closed for 18 months, the factory reopened in July 1888 as the Colchester Rubber Company.

This photograph was taken from Lebanon Avenue looking south along Mill Street. In the foreground at left is the Boot and Shoe Building of the rubber company factory (the same building shown in the previous photograph), with other factory buildings beyond it. In the foreground at right is the rubber company office building. This photograph is thought to date to shortly before the abandoned factory burned down in 1908.

In 1834, Nathaniel Hayward (1808–1865) started experimenting with natural rubber to try to improve its temperature-related properties. By 1838, he had discovered and patented a process for treating rubber with sulfur. He assigned this patent to his associate Charles Goodyear, who used it in his discovery of how to make vulcanized rubber. Hayward and Goodyear made an agreement to let Goodyear file for the vulcanized rubber patent while Hayward would be licensed to use it to make shoe products. Hayward died in 1865 and is buried in Linwood Cemetery with a grave marker in the form of a rubber tree.

In 1892, the Colchester Rubber Company was purchased by the United States Rubber Company. At the end of 1893, the factory shut down for its usual holiday break; without any notice, it never reopened, and the manufacturing machinery was later removed. The factory buildings remained empty and unoccupied until 1908, when a fire broke out in one of the buildings and completely destroyed the whole complex, as shown in this photograph.

The Jeremy River in the Westchester section of Colchester has had a dam and water-run mill of one kind or another since the 1720s. In 1886, C.H. Norton bought the existing paper mill and used it to make paper and paperboard products. In 1893, the mill burned down, and a new one was built. This picture shows the paper mill as it appeared in the 1920s. The mill went out of business in the 1960s and sat abandoned until 2016, when the owners sold the property to the town of Colchester for $1. That year, the town, in conjunction with the state, removed the dam, and the river ran free in this area for the first time in almost 300 years. The remains of the mill buildings have also been removed, and the property is expected to eventually be converted into a town park.

The Colchester Canning Company was incorporated on April 29, 1893, to manufacture and sell tin cans for preserving fruits and vegetables. The company's factory was built on Halls Hill Road, as shown in the 1899 photograph above that features plenty of cans ready for shipment. This company's timing was bad, however; the year after it started, the rubber company went out of business, and Colchester's economy collapsed. The canning company went out of business in 1905, and the building no longer stands. The below photograph shows the label from one of the Colchester Canning Company's sweet-corn cans featuring the "CCC" trademark.

Four

CELEBRATIONS
PARADES AND EVENTS

Everyone loves a parade, including the people of Colchester. The earliest known photographs of one in Colchester are from a parade in support of the United States' involvement in World War I.

A Memorial Day parade has long been a tradition in Colchester, and photographs from these parades date back as early as the 1920s.

Colchester's 250th anniversary was celebrated over three days in October 1949 and included a large parade and many other events. Since Colchester was incorporated in 1698, it is unclear why the 250th anniversary was celebrated in 1949 and not in 1948. In contrast, Colchester's 275th anniversary was celebrated in 1973, not 1974, and its 300th-anniversary festival was celebrated in 1998, not 1999. In any case, the 1949 celebration was a big deal and had a large attendance.

Other than pictures of parades, there are not many known photographs of events held in Colchester before the 1950s. The earliest example is a photograph of the dedication of a temporary memorial to those from Colchester who fought in World War I. Although it is not celebrated, probably the biggest single event to happen in Colchester in the 20th century was the hurricane of September 21 and 22, 1938. With sustained winds of over 100 miles per hour and even faster gusts, the hurricane did extensive damage in Connecticut and beyond. In Colchester, all able-bodied citizens were called upon to participle in the cleanup of the town, which took weeks to complete. This storm came to be known as the "Storm of the Century" and had an impact on Colchester that lasted for years.

The July 2005 issue of *Money* magazine named Colchester as the 57th best place to live in the country, and ever since, Colchester has celebrated that fact with a festival every September. Various organizations sponsor other annual events in town, such as the Colchester Lions Club's "Festival on the Green" in July. This event includes a colonial fife and drum muster featuring the Colchester Continental Fife and Drum Corps, which was formed in 2004 and modeled on an earlier organizaion from the first half of the 20th century (see page 123). The Colchester Lions Club also sponsors the ever-popular "Pumpkins 'N' Pooches Autumn Fair and Dog Fest" in October.

This picture features a parade during World War I. The poster on the side of the wagon reads "Buy US Government Bonds." The parade is heading north on South Main Street. In the background is the Morgan-Bulkeley House, which still stands at 219 South Main Street and is now home to a bank.

This image shows the Colchester State Guard marching in a Memorial Day parade around 1921. The parade is heading west on Norwich Avenue. In the background is the Wheeler House, which, by this time, may have become the Oliver Woodhouse Lodge of the Knights of Pythias fraternal organization. The building no longer exists, and the site is now occupied by a bank.

This photograph shows a parade marching north on South Main Street sometime in the 1930s. The marching band includes the Colchester Continentals Drum Corps that was the inspiration for a new fife and drum corps in the 21st century (see the chapter introduction on page 121). The first building on the right is Gates Hall, which contained the A&P Grocery Store on the ground floor and the Tip-Top Department Store on the second floor.

This parade is marching north along Merchants' Row in 1935. The band is unidentified. On the right side of the photograph, the following buildings are visible: the Worthington Block, with an appliance store and restaurant sign; the Scholl Block, with a soda shop sign; and the Roper Block, with tavern and barbershop signs.

This parade was marching north along Merchants' Row in 1949 as part of the celebration of Colchester's 250th anniversary. This image is similar to the previous photograph that was taken from almost the same vantage point 14 years earlier. In the background, Day Hall and the Colchester Federated Church are visible, and at right, the Worthington, Scholl, and Roper Blocks are visible on Merchants' Row.

The boy and girl dressed in old-time costumes were participating in the festivities associated with the 250th anniversary event held in Colchester in October 1949. The boy is pushing a carriage containing a doll, so they may have been taking part in a baby carriage parade event.

This is not really an event, but it is an interesting image nonetheless. This photograph shows the grading of South Main Street—with the use of a team of oxen—in the late 19th century. The paving of roads did not start in Colchester until 1927. Over time, unpaved dirt roads can become extremely rutty and require periodic regrading, as shown in this photograph.

This c. 1919 photograph is of the dedication of a temporary monument to Colchester men who fought in World War I. The ceremony was held on the small town green extension on Broadway. Around 1926, the temporary monument was replaced with the permanent one that is there today. The permanent monument has a plaque with the names of 93 men who served in the war.

In September 1938, a hurricane—later referred to as the "Storm of the Century"—hit Connecticut and Colchester hard. The hurricane was preceded by days of soaking rain that loosened the roots of many of the decorative elm trees that had been planted around town in the 1850s. When the high winds came, many of these trees were toppled. The above photograph is of South Main Street after the storm, with the Smith-Condren House and Colchester Baptist Church visible in the background. The below photograph also shows South Main Street, looking south, with Gates Halls visible at right. The road is flooded and blocked by downed trees.

ABOUT THE COLCHESTER HISTORICAL SOCIETY

The purchase of this book supports the Colchester Historical Society, which was founded in 1963 with a mission to enlighten the community to the rich history of Colchester. The society implements its mission by offering a variety of exhibits, programs, and events focused on local history. The Colchester Historical Society discovers, acquires, and preserves memorabilia related to Colchester and its residents. The society has also been instrumental in increasing awareness of the importance of preserving historic buildings in Colchester.

The Colchester Historical Society maintains a museum with exhibits pertaining to Colchester's history. The Colchester History Museum is located at 24 Linwood Avenue, adjacent to Cragin Memorial Library. For museum hours and other information about the society, visit the Colchester Historical Society's website at www.colchesterhistory.org. Thank you for your support. (Above, courtesy of the author.)

THE COLCHESTER HISTORICAL SOCIETY
PO BOX 13
COLCHESTER, CONNECTICUT 06415
www.colchesterhistory.org

Visit us at
arcadiapublishing.com

www.ingramcontent.com/pod-product-compliance
Lightning Source LLC
Chambersburg PA
CBHW082145150426
42812CB00076B/1913